on duty

LIFE IN THE
ARMY SPECIAL FORCES

Robert C. Kennedy

HIGH
interest
books

Children's Press
A Division of Grolier Publishing
New York / London / Hong Kong / Sydney
Danbury, Connecticut

Book Design: MaryJane Wojciechowski
Contributing Editor: Mark Beyer

Photo Credits: Cover, pp.24, 34 © Corbis; Side bar © Superstock; p. 5, 23
© Photri; pp. 7, 8, 10, 19, 31, 39 © Leif Skoogfors/Corbis; p. 13 © Peter
Russell/The Military Picture Library/Corbis; p. 15 © Michael S.
Yamashita/Corbis; p.16 © Annie Griffiths Belt/Corbis; p. 26 © Jim Sugar
Photography/Corbis; p. 29 © Catherine Karnow/Corbis; p. 32 © Alistair
Wright/The Military Picture Library/Corbis; p. 36 © Ricardo Watson/Archive
Photos; p. 41 © Reuters/Australian Defense Force/Corporal/Archive Photos

Visit Children's Press on the Internet at:
http://publishing.grolier.com

Library of Congress Cataloging-in-Publication Data

Kennedy, Robert C.
    Life in the Army Special Forces / by Robert C. Kennedy.
        p. cm. – (On duty)
    Includes bibliographical references and index.
    Summary: Explains how special forces soldiers are chosen and trained,
the different kinds of missions for which they are used, how special forces
teams are organized, and the specific functions they perform.
    ISBN 0-516-23350-5 (lib. bdg.) – ISBN 0-516-23550-8 (pbk.)
    1. Special forces (Military science)—United States—Juvenile literature. 2.
United States. Army. Special Forces—Juvenile literature. [1. United States.
Army. Special Forces. 2. Special forces (Military science)] I. Title. II. Series.

UA34.864 K45 2000
356'.167'0973—dc21
                                                                    00-024377

CONTENTS

Introduction

The U.S. Army Special Forces actually began with the American Revolutionary War (1776-1781). Back then, ordinary citizens were trained quickly as soldiers. These men were called Minutemen. They were taught to fight in small groups. These groups would hide behind trees and wait for the enemy. When the enemy was close, the Minutemen would attack. Then they would run away to hide somewhere else and wait. Minutemen also worked as civilians among the British soldiers who had captured cities. They counted the number of troops in a town. They also would overhear battle plans. Minutemen helped to combat the enemy undercover, as ordinary people.

Today's Special Forces use much the same system as did the Minutemen. However, the Special Forces are highly trained military personnel. They can sneak into and out of countries around the world. They can speak the lan-

*Revolutionary War (1775–1781) Minutemen
fought much like today's Special Forces soldiers.*

guage of the country where they are. They can
stop an enemy from harming innocent people.
They can quickly take people out of the country to safety. They also can be on the lookout
for the enemy and find out what the enemy
plans to do. Each of these missions takes place
in secret. However, Special Forces teams can
be a notable fighting force. Their job is mostly
one of secrecy. We almost never hear about
the work that Special Forces teams do until
years after they have done it.

What Special Forces Teams Do

Special Forces teams carry out many different kinds of missions around the world. They work both undercover and directly as military fighting units. Each member of a Special Forces team is trained in the language of the country to which their mission takes them. Each member also knows how to gather information (intelligence) by talking with local civilians or spying on enemy military forces. They are experts at communications, medical aid, engineering, and weapons. Their missions often require them to fight. However, they also serve to teach people how to fight for themselves. They train small troops in fighting. They also help such troops to understand warfare. The following are the kinds of missions that the Special Forces carry out.

Special Forces members help train friendly foreign troops for battle.

UNCONVENTIONAL WARFARE (UW)

Conventional warfare puts enemy armies against each other in the battlefield. Here, the enemies are lined up on opposite sides. The soldiers and machines fight to the death. Or, they fight until one surrenders to the other.

Unconventional warfare (UW) is much different. Small teams of soldiers move secretly in enemy-held areas. Such places also may be politically sensitive areas. UW teams fight guerrilla style (just as the Minutemen did). They attack the enemy quickly and then leave the area.

7

Special Forces teams must be able to sneak into enemy territory and stay hidden using camouflage uniforms and face paint.

UW teams help home troops or civilian groups try to overthrow a government. This is called subversion. Special Forces teams teach subversive groups how to organize themselves. Then these groups form political groups that work to gain power. Such groups also create anger among a nation's people. Sometimes, if enough citizens of a nation are angry with its rulers, they can change its government by force.

UW teams help people being sought by enemy governments to escape to safety. Such people include leaders of subversive groups.

UW Special Forces teams also try to destroy an enemy's army equipment. This kind of work is called sabotage. An example of sabotage is a team blowing up a communications tower. Sabotage upsets an enemy's ability to work well.

DIRECT ACTION (DA)

Direct action includes secret or open missions to steal, damage, or destroy a target. DA may require the Special Forces team to lead raids, ambushes, or assault plans. Or, DA may be more secret. A Special Forces team might tell a larger force where a target is behind enemy lines.

SPECIAL RECONNAISSANCE (SR)

Special Forces teams often sneak into enemy areas to gather information about an enemy or a target. This is a reconnaissance mission.

Special Forces soldiers use maps to find their way in enemy territory.

During such missions, intelligence is gathered to use against the enemy in the future. Such information includes enemy troop strength and battle plans.

FOREIGN INTERNAL DEFENSE (FID)

FID operations are ways to teach new governments how to manage their army and police. Such operations teach police and military new technical skills. These include computer, communications, and management skills. These groups also are taught how to treat their people fairly and humanely. Once a government is in power, it must help its people to earn a living and live peacefully. FID operations are an important part of the Special Forces.

COUNTERTERRORISM (CT)

Terrorists are people and organizations that are violently against a government. That government might be either their own or a foreign one. Terrorists bomb buildings, hijack planes, and kidnap people to make governments (and people) fear them. The Special Forces must fight against terrorists. Their CT operations are offensive missions to prevent terrorists from harming others. They are able to prevent terrorism when they have information about a terrorist or organization. If terrorists have already acted, the CT operation responds to the attack. The Special Forces team goes into an area and protects civilians against any further attacks.

OTHER SPECIAL FORCES MISSIONS

The Special Forces serve many other purposes than those just mentioned. These include:

- Influencing the way foreign governments treat their civilians
- Training civilian governments to work closely with their military forces
- Helping civilians or refugees adapt to conditions during or after a war
- Helping a variety of foreign military forces to work together during wartime

All that the Special Forces do begins with the individual soldier. However, not every soldier who wants to be a Special Forces soldier can become one. The Special Forces seek good soldiers who are able to become great soldiers, teachers, and fighters.

It takes the best to become a Special Forces soldier.

Choosing and Training a Special Forces Soldier

A Special Forces soldier can speak in at least one foreign language. He is strong. He is able to run, march, and swim for long periods of time. He's also creative, resourceful, and able to handle a high level of stress.

So how does the Army choose such a person?

HOW SPECIAL FORCES SOLDIERS ARE CHOSEN

The first thing the Army looks for is an experienced soldier. To apply for Special Forces training, a soldier must have four years in the Army and be in great physical condition. The Army Special Forces is a combat unit. By law, combat units do not allow women. If the soldier is not already a paratrooper, he must want to be one.

This is because Special Forces teams act in secrecy. The most secret way to get into an area is either to parachute in or to swim ashore from a submarine.

A Special Forces soldier must be able to move undetected through a jungle. He must be able to slide down a rope (rappel) from a cliff. He must be able to get deep into enemy-held areas. Once inside an enemy's area, he must be able to strike quickly and forcefully.

This kind of soldier is special. Only the strongest, most intelligent, and most highly-skilled soldiers are chosen to train. The Special Forces soldier is the best of the best.

Training includes rappeling down tall towers.

Special Forces trainees must learn to travel through all kinds of terrain.

SPECIAL FORCES ASSESSMENT AND SELECTION (SFAS)

If approved for Special Forces assessment, soldiers go to the Special Forces school. This school is located at Fort Bragg, North Carolina. Here, each soldier's physical and mental abilities are measured and judged. The assessment program lasts for four weeks. The program is given in three parts: phase one, phase two, and the "Q" course.

Phase One

Phase one measures a soldier's physical fitness, swimming ability, and how well he handles runs. Being able to run over different kinds of ground (terrain) is important for any soldier. A Special Forces soldier must be able to run over sand, ice, snow, rock, and jungle terrain. All different kinds of terrain running must be mastered.

Another program during phase one is the obstacle course. This shows how easily and quickly a soldier can move around and through obstacles. These obstacles are set up as they would be during a real mission.

Marching is also a part of the testing. Marches include carrying a backpack (rucksack) loaded with gear. The gear is food supplies, a tent, first aid equipment, and any special weaponry or gear.

Finally, military orienteering is a large part of any Special Forces mission. Military orienteering shows a soldier's skill in reading maps and using a compass to travel over land. Knowing how to get from one place to another can save a soldier's life.

A board of instructors decides whether an applicant has passed the phase one testing program. If he has, the soldier is allowed to enter phase two. If the soldier is rejected, he returns to the military position from which he came.

Phase Two

Phase two tests a soldier's leadership ability and how well he handles teamwork. This training has the soldiers doing practice missions in the field. They work as a team. Their teamwork shows how well they work together. These test missions also allow each soldier to show the kinds of jobs he does best. Such jobs include reconnaissance, demolition, infiltration, and orienteering. Completing phase two proves that a soldier is ready for Special Forces training. The next step is a specialty training course.

Group training teaches trainees to work as a team.

Q Course

Officers who have passed both phases go on to the Special Forces detachment officers qualification course (SFDOQC). Nonofficers (enlisted men) go on to the Special Forces qualification course (SFQC). Both are called the "Q" course. The difference between the two is that the SFDOQC course teaches advanced officer training. These courses train individual soldiers in specific skills. Such skills include weapons expertise, sabotage and underwater demolitions, and medical training. There also is training in communications and intelligence gathering.

19

The A Team

When a soldier is selected for the Q course, he begins training for a slot in a particular Special Forces operational detachment alpha (A team). When he graduates, he goes to that team and fills that slot.

SPECIAL FORCES ORGANIZATION

The A team is the building block of all Special Forces units. Each A team has twelve men. A detachment commander is in charge, and a warrant officer helps him. With the two officers, ten other highly trained special operations sergeants carry out the missions. Each man in the team can speak one or more foreign languages. Their special military skills are engineering, communications, intelligence, medicine, or weapons. Each team member knows at least two military skills. That way, if several men are too seriously hurt to do their jobs, the team still can complete its mission.

Detachment Commander

This is the captain of the A team. He must be able to plan and execute four of the five Special Forces missions. These are unconventional warfare, direct action, special reconnaissance, and foreign internal defense. The fifth Special

A Team Personnel

Detachment Commander	Captain
Executive Officer	Warrant Officer
Operations NCO/Team Sergeant	Master Sergeant
Intelligence/Operations NCO	Sergeant First Class
Weapons NCO	Sergeant First Class
Assistant Weapons NCO	Staff Sergeant
Engineer NCO	Sergeant First Class
Assistant Engineer NCO	Staff Sergeant
Medical NCO	Sergeant First Class
Assistant Medical NCO	Staff Sergeant
Communications NCO	Sergeant First Class
Assistant Communications	NCO Staff Sergeant

Forces mission is counterterrorism. Only a captain specially trained for this mission can be a counterterrorism team commander.

Warrant Officer

The warrant officer is the second-in-command of the A team. His job is to assist the captain. He also is the mission-planning expert for all Special Forces operations. Because of his expertise in how a team operates, he stays with one team for as long as possible. Therefore, the warrant officer is usually the team's longest-serving member. His most valuable skills are his knowledge of the culture (how people live), area, and language of the country to which the team is sent.

Weapons Sergeant

This A team member is the team's weapons expert. He is able to use, take apart, and repair most weapons used by any army. These include automatic weapons, mortars, pistols, and rifles.

All Special Forces members must be able to use different types of weapons.

Engineer Sergeant

This team member uses explosives to damage or destroy enemy targets. His expertise in sabotage and underwater demolition is important for the kinds of secret missions on which A teams are sent. Besides destroying targets, he also can build things such as bridges.

Medical Sergeant

The medical sergeant saves team members' lives. He has the most advanced field medical equipment available. Besides first aid, he can perform some kinds of surgery (operations). The medical sergeant also uses his medical knowledge to help civilians caught in war. These include refugees held in civil camps.

Communications Sergeant

The communications sergeant is responsible for electronic communications equipment. A communications sergeant is able to send and receive Morse code (a system of communication using no voiced words). He is able to operate, repair, and carry the different kinds of radios and communications equipment that a team uses.

Operations/Intelligence Sergeant

This sergeant knows how to gather information from civilians or the enemy. This information helps a team learn about things such as enemy strength and position. The operations sergeant tells the team captain how the information is important to the team mission.

Other Team Members

The remaining A team sergeants are assistants to the master sergeant or sergeant first class for specialty job duties. The team is outfitted with experts who know how to do their jobs, and how to train others to do such jobs. The A team is ready for a mission.

Each Special Forces team has a communications sergeant.

25

Special Forces Missions

The types of missions A teams are given have already been mentioned. However, for each kind of mission, an A team may do many different things.

A TEAM GROUPS AND FUNCTIONS

There are six A teams to a company, and three companies to a battalion. Three battalions form a group. A group is the largest number of men available for missions. In each company, one A team is scuba-trained and equipped. One A team is trained and equipped for high-altitude parachute entries (HALO/HAHO).

A teams often work together. However, each team may be used as a separate unit. For example, a Special Forces company may need to build a bridge across a fast-running mountain stream. Engineer sergeants design the

Some A Teams are trained for scuba missions.

bridge and plan how they will build it. The materials to build the bridge are collected. Then the company members and civilians build the bridge. When the bridge is finished, the company may leave one A team behind. This team trains the civilians in defending and repairing the bridge. The rest of the company moves on to the next mission. Because all teams have similar radio equipment, the stay-behind team can be contacted at any time. The team may be told to defend the bridge, or to move to a certain place for extraction (pickup).

The A team also may be ordered to split into two B teams of six men each. So, the A team becomes two self-contained fighting units. The captain commands B-1 and the warrant officer commands B-2. Each B team has the same skills as the full A team, but only half of the manpower and firepower. B-1 may stay to defend the bridge while B-2 moves to a better defensive position on higher ground.

Special Forces teams have an engineer sergeant who can plan and then carry out building a bridge.

Insertions

The first part of any mission is getting the team or group to the proper location. Getting a team or group to a certain place is called an insertion.

Teams usually are inserted by helicopter. For a jungle mission, teams may go into the landing zone (LZ) at treetop height and rappel quickly to the ground. However, some insertions have to be more secret.

Some teams jump out of an aircraft at 30,000 feet. At this height, they must use oxygen. These teams are called HALO/HAHO teams. HALO means high altitude, low opening. HAHO means high altitude, high opening. HALO teams jump at high altitude and open their parachutes when they are close to the ground. HALO teams are used in hilly or mountainous terrain. These teams are hidden from enemy view by the hills and mountains. HAHO teams jump from planes flying close to enemy

Special Forces teams are usually inserted into enemy territory by helicopter drops.

HALO/HAHO team members make parachute jumps from 30,000 feet.

territory. By opening their chutes high in the air, they can drift into enemy territory unnoticed.

HALO/HAHO teams use parachutes that can be steered toward a landing site. To hit the site exactly, the team memorizes satellite photos of the area where they are dropping. Using night vision goggles and a geographic positioning system (GPS), they are able to stay on course.

In January 1991, a Special Forces HALO/ HAHO team jumped into the northwest desert of Iraq. Their mission was secret, but it may have been to watch for Iraqi troop movements into an area where the mountain tribes supported the American invasion of Iraq.

Extractions

Once a mission has been completed, the A team or group must get out of the area. Getting out of an area is called an extraction. Most extractions are made by putting helicopters on the ground to load a team. Others are made using a military vehicle such as the Humvee, Bradley Fighting Vehicle, or a tank. However, extractions can get more complicated.

A chair lift device has been used successfully for many years. Here the passenger must be willing to take the ride. He straps himself into the chairlike frame and a helium-filled balloon attached to a very long rope is then let go. The

rope rises into the air for a few hundred feet. Then, a low-flying aircraft or helicopter snares the rope and hauls in the "chairborne" trooper. This system works great for extracting prisoners. The prisoner can be strapped securely into the chair. Then the balloon is released, and the chair is snatched into the sky.

PLACES SPECIAL FORCES TEAMS HAVE BEEN USED

Most missions are ordered by the president. Some are civic actions, such as capturing a person wanted for a crime. Others are military actions, such as sabotaging a communications facility. Still others are humanitarian actions, such as helping refugees relocate to safe areas.

In 1979, in Iran, American embassy workers were taken hostage by Iranian terrorists. Within days, Special Forces team members had sneaked into Iran's capital city, Teheran. They were ready to rescue the Americans. However, the terrorists separated the hostages into small

Special Forces units are taken out of enemy territory by hooking up to a helicopter line.

groups and hid them. The Special Forces team was unable to locate them. It was many years before all of the hostages were released.

In 1990, Special Forces were secretly sent into Panama. They were sent to capture General Manuel Noriega, the former president of Panama. When Operation Just Cause began, they moved in and forced Noriega's surrender. He later stood trial for drug trafficking and other crimes.

Special Forces teams also were used in Kosovo, Yugoslavia. Because of Serbian army forces attacking ethnic Albanians in the area, the civilians had to flee the country. Special Forces teams parachuted onto high ground during this conflict. They were sent to protect the thousands of fleeing refugees from attack.

Today, Special Forces teams are teaching African civilians to defend themselves against bandits who attack and burn their villages.

Manuel Noriega, former president of Panama, was captured by a special forces team.

THE FUTURE OF THE SPECIAL FORCES

Throughout the world there still exist small wars and battles between people and nations. Sometimes people are fighting within their own country. Other times, two or more countries are fighting against each other. These wars upset whole regions. Innocent civilians are caught up in these wars. These civilians must often escape their own countries in order to survive. The United States plays a special role in the world today because of its economic and military strength. Its military is often called upon to help people and countries around the world. However, huge armies are rarely used today. Instead, groups like the Special Forces are sent around the world because they are small. They are also highly trained in many different tasks. Therefore, the Special Forces will see much more action in the years to come.

In the future, Special Forces soldiers will be used in the world's hot spots.

LIFE IN THE ARMY SPECIAL FORCES

As the size of the U.S. military shrinks, the need for the Special Forces will grow. Their use will be felt throughout the world. They will be used in small and large operations. They will help foreign countries train their troops. They will teach foreign governments how to fight battles and wars. The special forces will also help civilian populations cope with these wars and battles. Once peace is gained, Special Forces teams help governments to rule their towns and countries by peaceful means.

U.S. civilians might not hear about Special Forces missions for months or years after they have been completed. However, we can be assured that A teams are out there somewhere helping people in need.

For secret missions, the U.S. military turns to the Special Forces.

New Words

A team the twelve-man building block of
Special Forces units

assessment measuring your abilities as a
soldier under physical and mental stress

B team one of two six-man units formed by
splitting an A Team

battalion three companies of Special Forces
A teams

civilian someone not on active duty in a
military, police, or fire-fighting force

communications sending radio messages,
by voice, Morse code and burst
transmission

company six A teams, with one SCUBA
trained and one HALO/HAHO trained

engineering the art of building bridges or
buildings

extraction a pickup, by helicopter, boat, land
vehicle or aircraft

group three battalions of Special Forces A
teams

New Words

guerrilla a small, armed force that attacks and then hides

HALO high altitude, low opening parachute entry into a target area

HAHO high altitude, high opening parachute entry into a target area

hostage a person held, by force, until certain demands are agreed to by someone else

humanitarian helping other people, such as giving them food or medical care

Humvee a low, wide, four-wheel drive vehicle for rough ground

intelligence information about an enemy and what he might do

Morse code communication system of dots, dashes and spaces invented by Samuel F. B. Morse

orienteering pinpointing yourself in strange areas, using available techniques

rappel to descend from a cliff or helicopter, using a rope alone or a rope and hardware

New Words

rucksack a canvas backpack used to carry
  gear while away from base camp
scuba self-contained underwater breathing
  apparatus
SFAS Special Forces Assessment and
  Selection program
SFQC Special Forces Qualification Course,
  known as the Q Course
terrorist someone who murders innocent
  people to scare others into obeying him
weapons all military weapons, American- or
  foreign-made, of any type

For Further Reading

Bown, Deni. *The Visual Dictionary of Special Military Forces.* New York: DK Publishing, Incorporated, 1993.

Chandler, Gil. *The Green Berets.* Danbury, CT: Children's Press, 1998.

Dunlop, Richard. Donovan, *America's Master Spy.* Chicago: Rand McNally, 1982.

Koons, James. *U.S. Army Rangers.* Mankato, MN: Capstone Press, Incorporated, 1996.

Leigh, Wade. *Assault on Dak Pek: A Special Forces A Team in Combat, 1970.* New York: Ivy Books, 1998.

Resources

Special Operations Recruiting

www.goarmy.com/job/branch/sorc/index.htm
This is the official Web site of the U.S. Army. Learn more about how to join the Special Forces. The site includes videos to view.

U.S. Army Special Operations

www.specialforces.net/army/special_forces/Defa ult.htm
This site gives information about different Special Forces groups. It also contains many links to other related sites.

Special Forces Association

P.O. Box 41436
Fayetteville, North Carolina 28309-1436
(910)485-5433
http://sfahq.org
Their goal is to advance the "principles and ideals of the Special Forces regiment."

Index

Index

About the Author

Robert C. Kennedy entered the U.S. Army at age seventeen and attended various specialized schools. He served with a military intelligence detachment during the Korean War and with a special operations detachment during the Vietnam War, in 1967. He ended his career as an instructor for the Military Intelligence Officer Advanced Course, which he helped to develop, in 1968.